Work Hard Playlist Hard

Work Hard Playlist Hard

The DIY Playlist Guide for Artists and Curators

Mike Warner

Published by Tablo

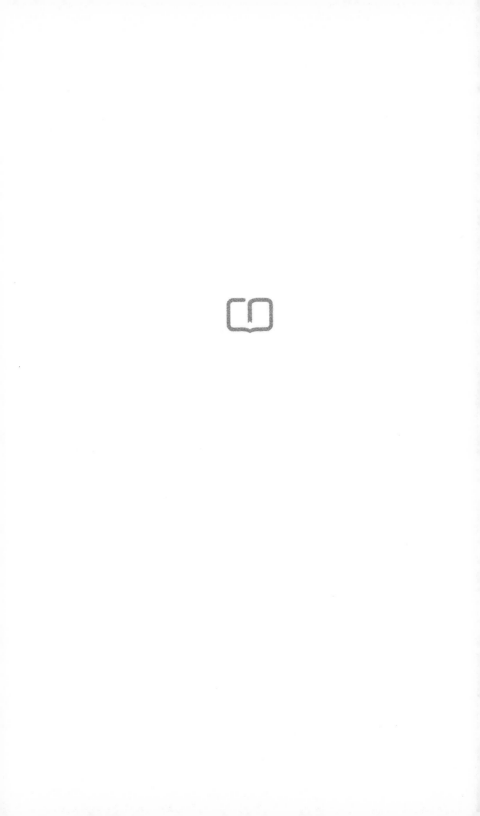

Table of Contents

Disclaimer

The information in this book is based on the author's personal experiences and should not be relied on for any purposes. It does not constitute advice or a recommendation of any product or service. Neither the author nor publisher accepts any responsibility for any errors, omissions or inaccuracy in the information or for any loss or damage that may result from reliance being placed on it. Products and services are constantly being developed and you should make your own enquiries before deciding how to proceed.

Introduction

Artists have more power, more tools and more knowledge than ever before. I've been a music lover my entire life, with a music collection of Funk, Hip Hop, Punk, Rock, Electronic, Ska and everything in between. I spent 15 years DJing, hosted multiple podcasts and radio shows, helped numerous artists become labeled as independent, produced music under various aliases and worked with a few background music services. After many years of trying to break into the music industry, applying to multiple jobs, I concluded that my resume wasn't strong enough... so I decided to build my own opportunities through self education.

This book details vital parts of my journey; from a keen music lover and starving music producer to a well fed streaming music nerd who makes a living in this beautiful, crazy industry. It is the result of many conversations with friends, artists, labels and managers. I suggest grabbing a pen and paper because I'll be hitting you with some things I wish I knew when I started out.

Many pieces of advice I share start with a question from an artist. This book is written as though I am telling a new artist how to set themselves up for success through the use of streaming services, all while building value in their brand through strong playlist curation.

❝

Tip: When you see text with Tip at the start (like this) pay close attention. These are short, quick, pieces of gold.

Set your goals

Goal setting should be common sense; if you don't have a goal, you have nothing to aim for and nothing to celebrate. For many years I wanted to be a world famous DJ and live out of a suitcase, clocking up frequent flyer miles and being a life member of an airport lounge. Rather than breaking up my end goal into smaller, obtainable targets, I was focused on the bigger picture. For example, I would need to develop unique skills, such as turntablism, while putting on an entertaining show that would draw bigger crowds each week, I would then need to push for becoming a support/warmup DJ for touring artists, find management... the list goes on and on.

It's safe to say, I didn't become a superstar DJ and tour the world. My priorities changed, I got a little older, and the idea of living out of a suitcase for countless nights, no longer held my interest.

I eventually got into producing electronic music with a good buddy of mine and realized that I wanted to focus my energy on creating and releasing music.

I wrote myself a new set of goals on the back of a scrap of paper. This time, I was more prepared. I set smaller, more realistic goals that would help me reach my end goal of becoming a producer. After one year the piece of paper was dirty, smelt terrible and could have been translated into digital form. Despite it all, I held onto it because it helped keep me accountable. I knew I wasn't going to recycle that piece of paper until every goal was crossed out. I don't have that piece of paper anymore as these goals have since been hit, but here is what it had scribbled on it:

- Release a full length album of music. 60 minutes minimum
- Collaborate with a talented vocalist
- Release a physical CD
- Play a headline show

These goals were all met; then new goals were created. It's important to always feel like you are accomplishing something, even if something like "have a top 100 song on Beatport" seems unachievable, write it down. When you cross a goal off your list, take a moment to celebrate, then get right back to grinding and working on the next one.

The next set of goals I created led me to where I am today:

- Work out how Spotify, Apple Music, and other streaming services work, become as close to a guru as possible
- Make strong contacts that curate large playlists
- Get featured on a Spotify editorial playlist
- Create my own playlist brand
- Make a living from music, whether it's producing, releasing, pitching, or a combination of things.
- Speak at numerous music industry conferences

"

Tip: Break your time up into blocks to allow 100% of your focus on a specific task. You'll find that by giving all of your focus to that one task it will be most likely be completed sooner. Use this spare time to stand up, take a quick walk, then come back and focus your attention on the next task.

How did I tick these goals off? How can you do the same? Follow the instructions in this book and you will be well on your way.

Types of playlists

There are different types of playlists, each playlist has value but how you approach the curators will change based on the type of playlist.

1. Editorial - Curated by staff who work directly for the streaming platform. These can provide significant streaming numbers but should not be your only goal as these curators rarely communicate with artists and their support is never guaranteed.

2. User - Also known as third party playlists. These are curated by an individual who has an account and has made their playlists public for anyone to follow and stream. Through making a connection with the owners of these playlists you may have a better chance of receiving future support on user created playlists.

3. Brand - A company profile with playlists, think Nike, Walt Disney, even celebrities can be verified with a brand account (influencers if you prefer). These are usually very hard to contact without knowing who at the company is in charge of the playlist.

4. Tastemaker - Very rare to see, in Spotify particularly when you go to a users profile, instead of saying "user" near their profile photo it will say "tastemaker". Rumor has it these tastemakers have earned this status through solid curation and artists have seen more editorial support after being added to a tastemaker users playlist. Coincidence or not, keep an eye out for these golden curators!

It's not uncommon for record labels to also curate their own playlists. The majors have their own playlist brands:

- Warner = Topsify
- Sony = Filtr
- Universal = Digster

Other labels will curate under their own name, the following electronic music labels have their own playlists for example:

- Walt Disney Records
- Spinnin
- Armada

Artist playlists can grow very quickly with the right network of supportive fans. The following artists have significant followings online.

Queen

5 Seconds of Summer

One Direction

Ed Sheeran

Notice that even artists that are no longer creating new music still maintain their playlists. It will always be a home for fans to enjoy their music, plus if the playlist has a significant following it is highly valuable to the artists manager/label who can include songs from similar artists in the playlist.

Let's get social

If you haven't already, sign up for the following social media accounts. If you are against social media, it's time to suck it up and accept that for many people in this industry it is the fastest way to make initial contact, forge a friendship, and maybe even get an invite to their birthday party.

- Facebook
- Twitter
- LinkedIn
- Instagram

Use the same username for all services. This is important for consistency and helping people find you. If you are @JohnSmithTunes on Instagram, then your Twitter handle should be @JohnSmithTunes - making it easy for others to directly tweet to you.

To keep it consistent, you should do a quick check on social media sites first by going to facebook.com/johnsmithtunes, instagram.com/johnsmithtunes etc. to see if the username has been taken (yes, you can do this from a web browser, much quicker than searching in the apps).

❝

Tip: If any new social media apps or sites launch after this book is released please also sign up for them, even if it is just to claim your unique username. If a new social media site takes off, you want to have facebook.com/johnsmithtunes not be stuck with facebook.com/johnsmith1989bro or worse. Claim it now, just in case! Here's a site you can use to check all socials at the same time - checkusernames.com.

Now, I'm not just going to tell you to sign up and then "get to work". Below are tips on creating a good profile, and where and how to find your first contacts. Once you've found them, don't do anything yet. Write them down on the piece of paper that you grabbed before.

Follow these GOLDEN RULES when creating profiles on social media.

Use your real name, even if everyone knows you by "DJ Smells Good." Don't give people an opportunity to decide what you are about until they connect with you.

Use a real photo of your face. Show that you are a real person, don't post crowd shots or a picture of the back of your head staring into the sunset.

Don't use fake credentials but, at the same time, don't undersell yourself. If you have been producing music for two weeks, don't include that, instead say "Music Producer. Australia". If people want to know more, they will slide into ask you.

Facebook

Facebook is a perfect icebreaker because you can easily see mutual friends of contacts, even before they accept your friend request. This gives you a chance to ask your mate if they know 'Person X' and if they could introduce you through a DM. Once the conversation has started and they have responded positively, then go ahead and send a friend request while you are speaking with them (they are less likely to ignore it if you are speaking with them at the time).

Twitter

Twitter is different. Introductions don't work, most people don't check their inbox or will block all Twitter users from being able to DM them. For now, set up your profile using the rules above and follow some artists, curators, or celebrities that you would like to work with or see inspirational tweets from. Once you have gained some value in yourself by creating your playlists (see Grow your playlist followings), then you will reach out to these Twitter contacts (if they don't hear about you first).

LinkedIn

While LinkedIn is mostly used for job hunting and co-worker creeping, it is also a useful tool for music industry professionals to network. Keep it real but also keep it relevant. Similar to Facebook, use an actual photo of your face (maybe a touch more professional here) and an honest resume. Also, only put relevant jobs, if you flipped burgers for five years but now work in a music store, just have the music store on your profile. Sign up for a free trial to get InMail credits. More detail on this in the Reach out to other curators chapter.

Instagram

You might be asking why you need to sign up to a website that consists of photos and videos. However, Instagram is a great place to reach out to social influencers (see Influencer marketing). No rules here, just post pictures that show who you are. If you love food, you'll fit right in but also share other cool stuff. If you went for a hike recently and saw a beautiful sunset, share it. People are more drawn to other people on Instagram, especially if you do cool stuff and post inspiring photos (don't post gig flyers unless it's the Coachella lineup and you are on it).

Set up your artist profiles

This is crucial. Even if you only have one song released, it's essential to have a profile with as much information as possible. If your song gets in front of the editorial team at a major streaming service they are going to look at your profile. If you have a photo, brief biography and an artist playlist, you have a better chance than the next artist that doesn't have anything on their profile. Below you will find links or details for the process for each streaming service. I intended to keep this chapter short and not copy/paste from the websites. You can find out more details once you sign up... so get to it.

Anghami

Anghami allows Artists to directly upload their music for sale, as well as offering analytics and payouts. Sign up at dash.anghami.com to set up your artist profile as well.

Apple Music

Register at artists.apple.com before you do anything else. This will give you insights into where your fans are from, as well as listener counts resulting from playlist adds. At the time of writing this, updating your Apple Music profile with a photo and biography is possible through your distributor.

Beatport

Beatport allow you to upload a professional headshot to your artist profile. The artwork must be at least 590 × 404 pixels and a JPEG image. You can do this by going to https://www.jotform.us/form/13105057250

If you are a DJ in addition to a producer you can create your own charts on Beatport at beatport.com/dj/charts/new and you can then add these charts to your artist profile.

Deezer

Email support@deezer.com with the subject "Artist Profile Update: Artist Name." In this email you can include two links to playlists you have created, these will be added to your artist profile as "artist playlists". Deezer also requires the URL of your artist profile (e.g., https://www.deezer.com/artist/6837) and your username (e.g., workhardplaylisthard) in the email.

Attach the following: a profile photo (a square JPEG image that is smaller than 3MB), links to your social media and an artist biography. It would be best to send them an email asking for the current image size requirements first.

Genius

A community of music lovers and artists sharing their knowledge and stories behind the music. Genius also deliver lyrics and extra information to various streaming services. You can get verified at genius.com.

Once verified you will be able to share accurate lyrics, hidden meanings/stories behind songs/song lyrics, and even to reach out to fans that are already annotating your music on the site.

Google Play

Google Play is shutting down at time of writing, this information is purely for historical purposes and for anyone wondering what happened to Google Play and what they offered.

Google Play allowed artists to take control of your artist page for a fee. Once signed up you would be able to claim your artist page, update the biography, images and genres for you music.

Google also provided the ability to sell your music directly and bypass a distributor, this would only work for music you own the rights to, which is totally fine if you are independent.

Once again this service is shutting down and being replaced by YouTube Music.

JioSaavn

Previously known as Saavn. Register at artists.saavn.com to gain access to data showing where your fans are from. A cool feature unique to JioSaavn is that it will show you other artists your fans also like and encourages you to collaborate with them on a future release to grow your fanbase together.

Napster

Napster only allows you to upload an image at this time. To do this send an email to support@napster.com. Be sure to include the URL to your Artist page so they know where to upload it. The dimensions for the image have to be 1500 x 1000 and a JPEG file. I found the team on their live chat to be quite useful https://help.napster.com/hc/articles/218661367

Pandora

Pandora has a useful Artist Marketing platform which allows you to place your own recorded messages alongside your music. This could be to promote an upcoming show or share a fun fact about your latest release. Sign up at http://amp.pandora.com to get access.

Qobuz

Qobuz is geared towards audiophiles, largely due to their integration with high end home audio equipment. You can change your artist photo by reaching out through the customer service portal https://www.qobuz.com/us-en/help/contact/ask/signin with a link to your artist page. Biographies and album reviews are written in house by the Qobuz team, and sourced from allmusic.com and Last.fm

Shazam

Sign up with Shazam for Artists and you will be able to update your profile with images, links to YouTube videos, as well as the ability to post status updates with links to new songs and have these displayed to any new fans that "Shazam" your song. Apple devices with Siri use Shazam as well, simply say "hey Siri, what song is this" if you don't have the Shazam app installed. Sign up at shazam.com/artists

Spotify

Register at artists.spotify.com and once verified, be ready to pimp your artist profile. Initially, you should at the very least have a photo, cover photo and biography. Especially because Spotify will sometimes send emails to followers of an artist, letting them know of a new release or upcoming gig in their city, they only do this for artists who have uploaded a photo. Also, while editing your biography you can type @ and link to an Artist, Playlist, Song or Album on Spotify in your biography. Can't find the right artist in the search results? You can type @ and paste the Spotify URI or URL directly after to make sure you link to the correct source.
e.g. @spotify:artist:2Yb3Wq5bwK9HNXvrLKsnVC

Tidal

Send an email to artistsupport@tidal.com with two photos, links to your social media, a short biography, and the URL to your artist profile on Tidal (e.g., tidal.com/artist/5124128).

YouTube Music

YouTube offers a wide variety of resources, including music video views by city and play counts over a chosen range of dates. There is a detailed blog and articles are published constantly. Sign up at artists.youtube.com

Create a great playlist

Playlists are one of the best ways to discover, share and rediscover music, so it only makes sense to want to have one of your own. Creating a playlist is the first step in creating something of value that you can use as leverage when reaching out to share music with other curators, but first let's make sure you have a great playlist. You have music, even if it is just one song. It's a great song and you'd like to see it added to some playlists so the first thing you need to do is to create a playlist that your song will fit into. Create a playlist featuring songs from artists similar to yourself, or songs from a specific genre. Stuck for ideas? Then think about:

- Artists that inspired you to write your latest single
- Songs that make you cry
- Songs you listen to while studying

Still stuck for ideas? Here's one more. Visit some of your local music venues and see which acts they are booking. After adding a few local artists to your playlists, make sure to reach out to them, letting them know you've added their music. You may find that once local artists begin to share your playlists their fans may start sharing it as well. You are a local artist too, there is no shame in adding your own music. Additionally, you are helping others in your local scene, which could lead to things outside of streaming, such as new gig opportunities.

Spotify search shortcuts

Spotify search is commonly used for finding songs, artists and playlists but there is so much more you can do. These search keywords are particularly useful when finding music from a specific record label, genre, release in a specific year, or range of years.

All of the keywords below are to be entered into the Spotify search bar. Type the bold text below into the search bar in Spotify to try this out yourself.

Search by label.
label: (record label name)
example - **label:universal**

Search by genre.
genre: (genre name)
example - **genre:rap**

Search by year.
year: (year or year range)
example - **year:2012** or **year:2012-2018**

You can add these together to create a more specific search. For example if you were curating a playlist of rap music released between 1990 and 1999 and through Tommy Boy Music you would enter the following into the search bar. Be sure to include : between each search keyword and a + between each word in the record label name.

example:
genre:rap:year:1990-1999:label:tommy+boy+music

You could use this to create a Best of 1990's playlist or even a playlist dedicated to your favorite record label and/or genre. By using these keywords you will be able to discover (or rediscover) many songs for your playlists.

In the search results you can then sort by artist name, or song title. This will help with the sorting process as you will see multiple releases featuring the same song.

Drag these into your playlist as you discover them, don't worry about order of songs just yet, just keep adding.

Curation

Now you should hopefully have a playlist of at least 50 songs (anywhere between 50-100 is ideal). Take your time here, put the strongest songs at the start. If you are doing a pop playlist, put some well known pop songs in the first ten tracks. Most people decide whether they like a playlist by pressing play and skipping through the first few songs, after this is when you can take a "risk" and add something the listener may not know, but again keep it relevant and make sure it fits with the rest of the songs on your playlist.

❝

Tip: Did you notice I only told you to create one playlist? This is because, once completed, you will focus your energy on growing the followers. I've seen artists make 20-30 playlists and then spend most of their "studio time" keeping them fresh. Keep it simple and do one playlist for now!

Artwork

Your playlists have to look as good as they sound. People see artwork before they click play so boil some coffee and crack those knuckles, let's get designing. If graphic design isn't one of your strengths, here's a tip: go to a website like Unsplash.com. Services like this enable you to download high resolution images and artwork royalty free. Once you have found a few images, go to Canva.com. For someone who has little graphic design experience, this online service is a great place to start. Canva has free templates and text fonts for almost everything - just drag your image in, change the text to your playlist name, and just like that, you look like a professional. If you have a small logo don't forget to include this in your artwork to raise awareness and maintain consistency with your branding.

Playlist description

This is where you "sell" your playlist to potential new fans. The description could be about all the "feels" people will be hit with once they press play, so tell a brief story in two sentences or less. It's also essential to include keywords. When you search for anything in Google, you type a few words to make sure you get the most relevant search results at the top. This is the same when searching for playlists in a streaming service. If your playlist contains music spanning five genres, then list all five genres in the description.

For the playlist title, make it something people want to hear and show some personality in it. "Songs I cry with my cat to", "festival season bangers" or "wild hens night" are clear descriptions of what to expect before clicking play.

Collaborative playlists

Most services allow users to create collaborative playlists. When shared, these playlists allow other users to add, remove and change the order of songs in the playlist. This is useful when creating a playlist for your band, as all members can add songs from their own devices. I used this to build the order for my debut album with my band. Please keep in mind that if these are public, anyone can find them and make changes, so keep the link and only share with trusted people. Always make backups of these playlists, to avoid losing hours of curation.

Tip: Create a second version of your most popular playlist as an archive. This will be a permanent record of all songs you have supported, artists can discover this long after you supported them in your main playlist and this will direct artists to your brand.

Host playlists on multiple services

Don't put all your eggs in one basket. You have a great playlist on Spotify. Why not push that same playlist to YouTube Music, Napster, Pandora, Apple Music, QoBuz, SoundCloud, Deezer and more?

Imagine how much more value your playlist would have if it was on all other primary streaming services. That's why I expanded my Spotify playlists to other services.

I guess you probably think it sounds like a lot of work, it isn't! Here are two services that will make your life a lot easier and save you from logging into multiple services each time you want to add a song to your playlist.

Soundsgood

This service has a web-based interface that allows you to automatically synchronize your playlists, including description and song order with adds/removals to multiple platforms. Artwork still needs to be uploaded directly to each platform but only once.

Soundsgood.co has an active community of curators and live chat, which are extremely useful when you are getting started. They also have unique URLs you can share which allow people to log in and stream your playlist on their desired streaming service, even if you don't have a profile setup on that streaming service.

Soundsgood also syncs the playlist order, so if you put a new song at the top of your playlist and remove some songs, it will sync the playlist order across all platforms. It is worth mentioning that this is only available through a web browser and there is no iOS or Android App available at this time.

Services currently supported:

Spotify, Apple Music, YouTube and YouTube Music, Naspter, Qobuz, SoundCloud, Deezer.

SongShift

SongShift is an iOS app for Apple devices. It offers more streaming services and also boasts an auto sync option (for paid subscribers). Auto sync works well for pushing new songs to playlists. Keep in mind this will only occur when the app is open but you will receive notifications telling you to open the app and sync your new songs. Song positions in playlists don't sync and song removals are not synchronized.

This app is good for a curator who wants to have their music on multiple services and won't ever remove songs from their playlist. I use SongShift to create a permanent back up of every song I have ever added to my Fresh Picks playlist.

Services currently supported:

Spotify, Apple Music, YouTube, SoundCloud, Deezer, Hype Machine, Napster, Pandora, Tidal, Discogs, Last.fm

Grow your playlist following

You have started to get a following on your playlists. People are listening, talking about and sharing your music and playlists. Now it's time to take it to the next level.

Social media shares

When you add a song to your playlist, kindly suggest to the artist that they share your playlist on their social media. In your message, you could have a friendly suggestion saying "Feel free to share the good news on your social media" then include your social links in your signature, so they can tag you.

Don't ever include your personal social media links in your signature, unless you want people hitting you up on your personal profiles.

You could go one step further and have a pre written Tweet that the artist could copy and paste. This way you can make sure they tag you correctly and have tagged the correct profile and used the correct links. Here's an example you can tweak to make your own.

Thanks @askmikewarner for adding me to your New Country playlist. Everyone go follow this playlist and give it a play.

open.spotify.com/playlist/3JNbSnDJWgb3gwUTHigP7f

❝

*Tip: Spotify have developed a great way for you to share your
Spotify information with fans or other artists, by using special
codes. Visit SpotifyCodes.com to find out about how these codes
can enable you to share information and create marketing
materials.*

Live stream

Facebook, Twitter and Instagram all allow you to "go live" to
your followers. Use this to host a live stream listening session
about your playlist. Post your submission link in the comments
and encourage live submissions and real time engagement.
This shows you are a real person listening to submissions. By
doing so you are likely to see the number of engagement and
submissions increase.

❝

*Tip: Get more viewers while you are live by sharing Facebook
live videos to groups. People in these groups receive instant
notifications in Facebook, which will also notify users of the
Facebook App on their mobile device. Where possible, encourage
friends and supporters to also share your live videos to their
groups for maximum news feed exposure.*

Post playlist artwork

Post playlist artwork on Facebook, Twitter, and Instagram.
Tag all new artists whose music you have added that week. At

the very least you will get a 'like'. Some artists may even reach out and ask for your email to send you more music if they happen to also curate playlists. Either way it is a win win as you have a new connection.

Short links

Use a URL shortener to turn those long URLs into something short and easy to share. Here's a few useful sites.

sptfy.com - Shortens Spotify links for Artist, Album, Song or Playlists e.g. sptfy.com/coconutkids (links to artist profile)

Bit.ly - Shortens any link to anything on the web e.g. to your artist website, a youtube video, social media, anything online e.g. bit.ly/2H9OQXj (links to submission form on Work Hard Playlist Hard website)

Toneden.io - Creates a fanlink to share your album, playlist and social media all on one page. Users can choose their favorite streaming service and it will direct them to your pro-file or playlist on that streaming service automatically e.g. fanlink.to/datenight (links to artist profile on all streaming services).

These services offer a number of added benefits including click tracking, which means you can see how many people followed your link and where they came from. The other benefit of having a short link is for posts on services like Instagram, who don't allow clickable links in the photo description. For example, you can type in a short URL that's easy to remember - allowing users to manually type it into their web browser.

Gates

A gate is a way to offer something in return for an action. One example could be offering people a free download of a song, e-book (grin) or something else of value, in return for a social action - such as following a channel on YouTube, following a playlist on Spotify, or sharing a tweet, etc. You can create a gate using services like show.co or toneden.io

You could also create your gate by hiring a developer through a website like Upwork.com - as always, do your research first and make sure your gate complies with the terms and conditions of your relevant streaming service.

❝

Tip: Use a gate to grow your Spotify followers. You will notice that the more followers you have, a higher amount of streams will come through via 'Release Radar'.

Marketing tools

Streaming services want you to share links to your profile, playlists and music on their platform. They also want you to look good while doing it. Here are the current marketing websites for these streaming services that allow you to create banners, widgets and custom links to share your releases on your website or social media.

Apple Music/iTunes
tools.applemusic.com

Deezer
developers.deezer.com / musicplugins / player

Spotify
developer.spotify.com / technologies / widgets /

Tidal
embed.tidal.com

YouTube Music
developers.google.com / youtube

Pitch your music to curators

Now that you have value in your playlists, you might find that other curators become more receptive to your emails. Ask permission before sending music, showing respect from one curator out to another. If the curator is also an artist or record label and you add one of their songs to your playlist this is a great ice breaker. Of course, be a good curator and only add music that is a good fit in your playlists.

Think about it. How many times per day do curators receive emails that start with "I'm sure you get a lot of these emails..." just stop! You aren't going to stand out if your approach is the same as everyone else. You are reaching out to an artist (or record label) that is also a curator. Open by telling them the following, in this order:

1. You added their song to your playlist. Link.

2. You would like to hear more music from them, invite them to add you to their mailing list or send you new songs directly.

3. That's it.

"I didn't ask them to listen to my music, and I didn't even tell them I'm an artist." That's right, this isn't about you, this is about them! Send a nice email, LinkedIn InMail, or Facebook DM.

If they don't respond within three days, post on Twitter/Facebook, share your playlist publicly and tag the artist, saying something about why you like the song and why everyone needs to hear it. Lastly, mention it was added to your playlist and include a link.

If this doesn't work, repeat for the next single from that artist. Keep doing this. If you add 20 songs by 20 artists you like to your playlist, you may only get one response. Imagine if you add 100 songs to your playlist, which is five new relationships starting to flourish.

Once you have a direct line to the artist, start out by having brief, fun conversations. This will be a relief for them and you may find they will even start writing to you randomly to get something off their chest, or to tell you about their fun weekend.

Now you have built some rapport, send an email with the following in this order.

1. Hey (name), followed by one sentence of friendly banter so they know it's personal.

2. I have added your new song to my playlist, and I've included details below.

3. But first, I've meant to ask if you are open to receive the occasional song submission from me for your playlist consideration. Let me know as I've got a new single coming out that would fit your XXXXXX playlist.

4. Lastly, here's the link to my playlist, I added your track to the top and will share the news on social media today.

Organization is key

Once you get a "yes", start building your database. It's important to note the following details.

- Name

- Preferred genres

- Submission lead time (private link before release or spotify uri/url once released)

- Where to submit (do they prefer email, message on Facebook, text etc)

- Link to their playlist profile (you don't want to have to keep asking "where can I find your XXXXXX playlist".

- Phone (some curators may ask you to text them).

- City, Country (incase you have travel plans, grow the friendship in person).

Reach out via LinkedIn

A free trial with LinkedIn gives you InMail credits which let you message people even if you aren't friends. InMail messages are taken more seriously because you have "spent money" to send that message as it goes to the top of the recipient's inbox. Search for playlist curator or playlist editor.

❝

Tip: Search for interns at record labels/playlist brands on LinkedIn. Interns are usually found proudly displaying their job title and email address on LinkedIn, which makes them easy to find and interact with. They tend to also be more responsive to InMail messages.

Find curators using Chartmetric

Chartmetric lets you sift through almost every playlist / curator on Spotify, Apple Music, Amazon Music and Deezer. You can filter out Editorial playlists, only seeing independent third party playlists. You can also filter to only see curators who have added their social media URLs - making it easier to narrow down your search for ways to make contact.

''

Tip: When reaching out to a curator, do not include any song links in your message. Ask them if they have a submission process and when they respond with the process thank them and follow their instructions. This will earn you instant respect from the curator because you asked them how to submit music to them instead of cold pitching, like 100's of other people are doing every day. Ask permission, show respect, say thank you.

Pitch via your distributor

Pitching your music correctly is a fine art that takes time to master. The good thing is that you are not alone, here's one method for getting your music in the front of editorial teams at streaming services.

While this information may not be in big neon lettering on your distributor's website, you may find that through some research (or by flat out asking them) your distributor has contacts at most major streaming services that they pitch to. Now, why wouldn't distributors advertise that they have these connections? Because they have thousands of new releases uploaded every week. If they offered this as a service on their front page, every artist would send them a "pitch." This is why you have the upper hand. You are educated, you have great music, and you are prepared.

Now, approaching your distributor is the same as approaching a curator, don't hit them with a pitch! Ask if they have a submission process for consideration of upcoming releases to forward to their editorial team contacts at streaming services.

Important things to keep in mind:

- Distributors get lots of direct emails so be patient and give them a few days before following up.

- If you still don't get a reply try another contact method, look for their artist/label relations contacts on LinkedIn and reach out with a brief friendly message.

- Distributors need lead time, just like editorial teams at major streaming services. Give at least four weeks minimum before your release date. Meaning if your song comes out April 29th, you should email them in mid March to be safe.

Pitch directly to the Spotify

Spotify submission forms have been floating around the web for some time now. For the fortunate few artists that located these mysterious Google Forms, the links were closely guarded and rarely shared. With major labels and distributors able to pitch priority releases to the Spotify editorial team through other means, many independent artists expressed their feelings of being left out in the cold. Now, all users of Spotify for Artists or Spotify Analytics, have the opportunity to submit a song to the relevant editorial team (i.e. genre, mood, etc.).

If you have an upcoming release (a song that has been uploaded via a distributor but is not out yet), you will see an option at the top of your dashboard allowing you to submit a song. If your upcoming release is an album, you will only be able to submit one song from the album.

SUBMIT A SONG will appear on the top right corner of your dashboard. This will soon relocate to the new Catalog screen, then under 'Upcoming'. This will only show if you have an upcoming release.

Once you submit a song, Spotify will ask you to add details relating to genre and sub genre. You can also share mood, moment, and even the location associated with your release.

One very important (and exciting) piece of information that seems to be overlooked, is that your song will be added into the Release Radar for ALL of your followers if you submit at least 7 days before release day. Previously some artists noticed their new song releases were not included in Release Radar for all of their fans (sometimes even missing Release Radar entirely).

Again here's what's great about this. If you have 5,000 followers, that equals 5,000 Release Radar playlists that your song will be added to that week! If you've submitted for playlist consideration at least 7 days in advance, your track will automatically be shared to your followers' Release Radar playlist on release day. This means the number of followers you have equals the number of Release Radar playlists your song will appear on the Friday of the release.

Songs that are submitted fewer than 7 days in advance are not guaranteed placement on Release Radar. It's also worth noting that if you do a separate release for a remix of your song it is not guaranteed Release Radar placement, only original songs uploaded for the first time will be.

Paid pitching services

If you don't have the time or need a break from pitching, there are a number of services that will do the job for you. These services vary in price and offering. Do not take these as recommendations as the services provided are subject to change without notice. Instead, consider this as an outline of the kinds of services that are available.

Crosshair: At time of writing, campaigns cost $250 each, with a discount for multiple campaigns. All curators are paid once they have listened for at least twenty seconds without skipping through the song, feedback and a rating out of 5 is also required. If a curator chooses to support your song there is a messaging system where you can chat with them to say thank you and perhaps get their social media details to post a public thank you.

Playlist Push: This is extremely detailed in comparison to other services, but it comes at a premium price for larger campaigns. Playlist Push actively removes playlists with low monthly listeners and also bans "purchased" playlists that have large follower counts but no listeners. A nice touch here is that curators are given a 'follow' button and encouraged to follow artists whose music they like. The process to add a song is easy and curators may be more likely to add due to how simple it is.

SubmitHub: A service that was created by Jason Grishkoff, who runs a blog called IndieShuffle. SubmitHub allows you to pitch to independent Spotify playlist curators, blogs and

YouTube channels. If you get stuck, there is a live chat room on the site with artists, curators and SubmitHub staff available to answer your questions. There are both free and premium submissions, which are achieved by purchasing credits. For premium submissions, if a submitter does not receive a response within 48 hours, a refund in the form of submission credit is honored.

Playlist pluggers

There is an insanely large number of "playlist pluggers" and "Spotify PR" companies out there. Do your research, ask to see songs they've recently worked on, then ask those artists if these companies did run a PR campaign for them and if they were satisfied. It's common for an artist or label to pay multiple playlist pluggers, and then only continue to work with the good ones.

If something sounds too good to be true, it probably is! A few warning signs to look out for include free email accounts (@gmail, etc.) and/or no trace back to any team members on the website. You can also look them up on LinkedIn to see if they have real people working for them, look at their fan page on Facebook and see if any of your friends like the page (then ask them if they have used their services).

Lastly, you can comment on sites such as Reddit (an online forum), asking if anyone has used them before. If people have had a bad experience they will gladly speak up to save someone else from being ripped off.

Background music services

Ask your parents (or maybe even grandparents) what MUZAK is, you'll be suprised. This is not a new thing. Background music (in-store or overhead music) has been around for many many years. Fortunately music has evolved from "elevator music" to feature various music from independent to established artists. This is "free money" as I like to say. Most background music services will only add music that is directly licensed to them, meaning the only way to get your music played in stores they service, and to get paid for that play, is to license your music to them. This doesn't mean that they own your music, it means they have your permission to use it (read the contract, of course, to make sure this is the case).

Imagine shopping in Macy's and hearing your song blasting through the speakers, and seeing someone whip out their phone to Shazam the song that is playing. This additional exposure can lead to a growing fanbase on Apple Music and Spotify. The app now allows you, as a user, to directly stream songs previously Shazamed, in full (counting as play), while adding to your 'My Shazamed tracks' playlist on either service. Lucky for you, you already set up your Shazam profile earlier in the book, right?

To get you started I have listed a selection of background music services that have previously accepted submissions from myself. Reach out via their general email on their web-site, first asking for their music submission process. Once you have the correct contact/ email, then follow up with your most recent single only. If they like your latest single and want your whole back catalog of music, they will ask you. Don't send everything in the first email.

Mood Media (Global)

Nightlife Music (Australia and New Zealand)

PlayNetwork (USA)

RX Music (USA / Canada)

Soundtrack Your Brand (Global)

Stingray Music (Canada and Australia)

StorePlay (Australia)

YouTube channels can grow your followers

There are some brands on YouTube with millions of followers. These channels are the result of one single curator, or a team of curators spending countless hours sourcing amazing music, engaging with their audience and building an organic following. These channels have built a large amount of trust through uploading great music. It's no surprise that many of these YouTube channels have ventured into the world of record labels.

Since these YouTube channels are launching their own record labels, it makes sense that they are building a following on music streaming services, especially with their own playlists. There are two ways that YouTube channels are promoting their playlists and your profile.

Description

In the description under the visuals you may see links to the channel's Spotify playlist, the artist's profile, as well as social media.

Gates

Many of these YouTube channels will also offer a free download of a song, and include their playlist in the gate. Ask them nicely if they could also add your streaming profile in the gate. Given that the free download recipient has already decided that they want your song, and they like the channel they discovered it on, following you on a music streaming service should not be an issue. They get free music, you get a new fan, and the channel builds their following on another service.

Making contact

Best methods for contacting YouTube channel owners can vary. Here are some suggestions on how to make first contact.

- In the about page on the YouTube channel, if listed there will be a button to "view email address".

- Locate the Facebook fan page for the channel, if they are open to receiving messages you can reach them here.

- Twitter allows you to Tweet the channel owner, if they have allowed DM's you can also make contact through this method.

- LinkedIn - InMail message

- SubmitHub - free or paid submission

Before reaching out, take a look on the curators profile to see if they mention a submission process. If they say, "only submissions through email will be accepted", respect their wishes. This means opting out of sliding into their DMs on Twitter.

Hype Machine

Hype Machine has been around since 2005 and is still referred to by many of my colleagues as their "go to" for finding new music that has yet to hit streaming services. You see, Hype Machine pulls data from 100's of active music blogs and formulates it into charts. All songs are embedded from SoundCloud links, which means artists can upload music to SoundCloud even before it is released, in which case a blog would premiere the song.

It's also a little known fact that some editorial team members at streaming services also subscribe to various music blogs and look to Hype Machine to find new artists that need to be discovered. Personally I have seen a few artists charting on Hype Machine, then added to popular discover playlists such as "Fresh Finds", the following week. While not saying this is definitely going to happen, it's safe to say that being on Hype Machine will increase your chances of the right people hearing your music.

Now being listed on Hype Machine is not achieved by sending them a "pitch". The only way for your song to appear on the site is for one of these blogs to write about your song - https://hypem.com/sites.

You could go through the above list and work through every single blog, contacting them individually and using your charm to try and get them to check out your song. Keep in mind that there are many artists using the same method, so for every 200 emails you send, you may get 5 responses and possibly only one blog feature. If this isn't soul crushing for you then I highly recommend taking the time to do this.

In SubmitHub you have the option to filter the blogs, by genre, as well as only seeing blogs that are on Hype Machine. This means that you are now only focusing on blogs that could get you added to Hype Machine (if they write about your music).

Make money as a curator

You have a playlist with a following which probably means people are reaching out to you on social media or emailing you their music. Why not make some money while you are listening through these submissions. Below are a list of websites that welcome curators to sign up and pay you for listening to submissions and giving constructive, useful feedback.

Crosshair - This service offers paid campaigns to artists for a fixed fee. For highly active curators who give strong feedback and respond within the required time, Crosshair can pay anywhere between 0.25c to over $1 per submission.

SubmitHub: Having both a free and premium option, this credit-based service allows submitters to choose specific curators to send their music to. As a curator, you get paid for responding to every premium submission you receive within 48 hours.

Playlist Push: For a varying fee, based on genre and number of curators a song is sent to this service offers paid campaigns to artists. Curators have two weeks to respond and are monitored heavily to make sure their playlists have engaged listeners. Curators are rewarded a higher payout per submission review based on their following, engaged listeners, feedback value and how long they leave an artists-song in their playlist.

Be aware of websites that suggest you take payment in place of adding a song. This is payola. Just don't do it; see the Payola chapter for more details.

Protect yourself

Now that you are growing (whether as an artist, curator, or both), you have something of value in your fans, followers and your brand. You need to protect your social media profiles from hungry hackers who want to take over your fan page or delete your account (yes, there are some mean people out there that do this). Don't panic though, there are plenty of things you can do to make sure you protect all of your accounts. Follow these steps.

Passwords

Change your passwords yearly and never use the same password again. Use a different password for each site. If someone gets your Facebook password and it also happens to be the same password for your internet banking, then you could find yourself broke one day.

Don't save passwords in online documents. It's safest to assume that nothing stored online is safe. Buy a notebook, write them all down, and put that notebook in your safe!

Use long passwords as hackers use bots to cycle through password combinations until they guess your password. The longer your password, the longer it will take them to guess, by then you would have already changed your password.

Two factor authentication is an extra layer of security. In addition to entering your password, a short temporary password is sent to your phone and is also required to be entered before you can log in to your account.

App/website logins

Remember all those websites that allow you to login with your Facebook account. Well, if someone hacks into your Facebook, guess what they also have access to all of the apps you've synced your account with? This also applies to Google and other accounts. Whatever platform you use, search the help center and find out how to remove unnecessary third party logins / apps that have access to your account.

Create music for playlists

Curators add songs that fit into their playlists, meaning the song matches a specific feel, genre, or style with the rest of the songs in the playlist... with an exception of longer tracks to keep the listeners interested. Think about radio edits of songs: they are short and to the point. This is for time management and to keep the audience from changing stations - The same principle applies to playlists. This is why it is important to release a short version of your song specifically catered for playlists. Now before we proceed please don't let this ruin your creativity or originality, finish the original unmodified version as intended and then work on a short edit that is geared towards fitting into playlists.

Make a short version that will fit in popular playlists with other short songs (also known as radio edits). Look at popular playlists on Spotify with similar music to what you are releasing.

Listen to it and take note of the following:

- Song length (best to keep this under 4 minutes)
- Intro length (less than 15 seconds, or people may skip before the 30 second mark)
- Outro length (less than 15 seconds, you want people to let your song play all the way through)
- Song structure (start with the main hook, vocal, or something that lets people know what your song is about in the first 15 seconds).

It's important to know that playing a song only counts as a stream. If people listen for more than 30 seconds, that stream is tallied for (yes, you get paid for it). If they listen to your song for less than 30 seconds it doesn't count as a stream and you don't get paid. You need to grab their attention early so they don't skip, then hold their attention at least past the first 30 seconds (and hopefully for the rest of the song).

This will give you an idea of what to do for your edit. Again, don't let this ruin your creativity. Finish your song first, then make an edit. You can include both versions by releasing the radio edit first, as a single, then save the extended version (with your epic intro) for the album.

❝

Tip: Take the long intro for your song and make it into a separate track. If someone skips the intro, your song will play next. However, if someone listens to your intro, then your song, this is two streams (one for the intro track, one for the song). For an example of this you can look up Date Night's self-titled album https://open.spotify.com/album/2qqqqSuv2iKyfUdxn8yWrM. Keep in mind that for an intro or interlude track to also generate streaming revenue (sales) it must be at least 30 seconds long.

It's one thing to create a short version of your song, but if you want to potentially make a living from playlists, your next step is to create music for the curator. This is not for everyone as it can be a huge blow to creativity but for some artists with a very niche market this may be worth trying out. Let's take

Lance Allen for example. Lance is an extremely talented guitarist and has built a large following through his beautiful guitar covers and acoustic original productions. Initially, he got lucky with the Spotify algorithms, but this wasn't enough for Lance.

Instead of sitting on his hands to wait and see if Spotify would support his newest single, Lance decided to approach independent curators with large followings, for himself. His next step, however, was pure genius.

Lance didn't pitch his song to the curators, instead he asked them what they are looking for when considering song additions! Now, this is the best way to get a curators attention, instead of telling them what you want, you ask them what they are looking for.

Let's say that curator A responds with "I'm looking for an acoustic cover of the new Bruno Mars song, I love the song but my playlist is strictly acoustic covers". Lance could then go and record this, knowing that once the song is created there is a very good chance this curator will be adding it to their playlist, especially knowing it was created specifically for them.

Yes, Lance is a guitarist but this could apply to a singer/songwriter, band, and even someone that can play one heck of a pan flute. If you have a niche audience, I am sure these curators would love to hear from you while supporting your releases.

Collaborate with other musicians

There are many benefits to collaborating with additional artists on a song. You could achieve a different sound, or simply bring on a guest vocalist. The result can be unique and potentially loved by both your audience and theirs.

The best part of this comes when releasing your music. Not only will the song hit your audience, it will also hit theirs. If you have 1,000 followers on Spotify and they have 1,000 followers, you have potentially doubled your audience for the track.

To make sure you reach all followers you need to have both artists as a "main artist". If you have one artist as "featuring" it won't reach their audience or necessarily show on their profile as one of their releases.

If all artists involved are actively promoting, sharing and pitching the release you have increased your chances significantly.

If you start a new project under a new alias, or a collaboration, you don't have to lose your followers. One example is Diplo and Mark Ronson, both have huge follower counts. They started a project called Silk City (which had no followers initially). Their debut single had three main artists tagged Silk City, Diplo and Mark Ronson.

This meant that the debut single from their new project would hit all of the combined followers for the three artist profiles. With a follower count in the millions and guaranteed Release Radar placement if submitting more than 7 days prior to release, this makes for a successful release, regardless of what additional support they receive.

ISRC codes and your release

The International Standard Recording Code known as ISRC, is used to uniquely identify sound recordings. Whenever you release a song through a distributor an ISRC will be generated. These are extremely important if you intend to release a song as a single, then also include it in an EP or album. In this example I refer to the single 'Sick Boy', from the Chainsmokers.

Now, the Chainsmokers already have a huge following so naturally this song received millions of streams within it's first two weeks of release. Here's the clever bit. A few weeks later they released their next single 'You Owe Me' and included Sick Boy on that release. The release was titled 'Sick Boy... You Owe Me'. When uploading the second release the original ISRC for Sick Boy would have been added. What did this mean? On the day the release went live, you could look at the stream counts for Sick Boy and it already had millions of streams. This is the ISRC piecing everything together.

But, they didn't stop there. A few weeks later another single was released 'Everybody Hates Me'. This time they included two extra songs in the release, 'Sick Boy' and 'You Owe Me'. The release was titled 'Sick Boy... Everybody Hates Me'. Surprise, surprise on the first day the release stream counts for 'Sick Boy' and 'You Owe Me' were huge.

Aside from building up stream counts on a song through multiple releases as detailed above, this is also a useful tool to build traction for an album. You could release a song every week or two weeks and give each song a chance to shine in Release Radar, Discover Weekly and other playlists, then give them another chance when the album is released. Look at other major artists like Diplo, Calvin Harris, Justin Timberlake... you can tell they have an album coming when you see multiple singles released in a calendar month.

While your fan base may not be as big as these artists, there is nothing stopping you to use these tactics while you grow your fan base. E.g. You have 100 followers when you release your second single, 500 followers when you release your third single and so on.

Go to any streaming service, look at the top 10 songs for an artist. If you see one instance of a song in the top 10 and you know that artist has released that song multiple times (perhaps including a remaster) then it is likely to be the result of using the same ISRC.

On the flipside, if you see the same song multiple times in an artists top 10 songs, it is likely they changed distributors and put the song out again not using the existing ISRC code. This means one song could show multiple times in your top 10, leaving less room for other songs.

To see how this was applied, follow these links and notice that the stream count is merged across all three releases:

the Chainsmokers - Sick Boy
https://open.spotify.com/album/2QI0UclC8ipuXoyCva1C7K

the Chainsmokers - Sick Boy...You Owe Me
https://open.spotify.com/album/7ipPGzgSu86WmYyNyx2Kr y

the Chainsmokers - Sick Boy...Everybody Hates Me
https://open.spotify.com/album/6Ok0x408eB6DmOrp13Llu3

Related artists on Spotify

If you visit an artist profile on Spotify and look at the Fans Also Like tab, you may be wondering how these related artists are being generated. According to Spotify the Fans Also Like tab on your artist profile is determined by algorithms, using a combination of your fans' listening habits, music discussions and trends happening around the internet.

If you've recently had your music added to Spotify or perhaps you have had to request a separation of your music from an artist with the same name, there is a good chance that your Fans Also Like artists are way off.

For instance, I once worked with a house music producer who shares a name with a children's singer - for obvious reasons, he swiftly wanted to correct his related artists. To correct the related artists, Thomas Garcia, signed up for an account with last.fm. The next step was logging into last.fm, going to settings, then applications and opting to connect for Spotify Scrobbling and Spotify Playback.

Last.fm will keep track of your listening history within Spotify and will automatically start to piece together other users listening history. My suggestion would be to create a new playlist, say 20 or 30 songs long, including music from both the artist and similar artists you'd like to be related with. Next, share this with some friends or fans and ask them to play it through once or twice (only once or twice, no cheating the system unless you want to get blacklisted). Just make sure your listeners log into their last.fm account and connect to Spotify first.

If all goes well, as it did in my experiment, within a few weeks you should see your related artists start to change and hopefully be more relevant to your music.

Pre-saves are the new pre-order

Remember when pre-ordering an album from your favorite band meant visiting your local record store and leaving your name and phone number to secure a physical copy?

As the robots took over and technology advanced, people started purchasing their music through iTunes and more recently Amazon and Google Play. This prompted the need for pre-orders to move from record stores to online sales. The benefit of a pre-order on iTunes, for example, was that people could pre purchase your song - meaning that once the track has been released, it would appear in the purchasers library. The best part for an artist is that all of the pre-orders are counted on day 1. This means that all the "sales" over the weeks leading up to that release are all calculated on release day. This strategy is how many labels and artists would have a "number 1 on iTunes on release day", although they may go quiet in the days that follow.

With iTunes rumored to phase out downloads in the near future, it's time to plan ahead. This is where pre-saves come in.

A pre-save is usually delivered in the form of a gate (see Gates). It encourages fans to follow a simple action and in return be one of the first to hear an artists' new single. To set up a pre-save you will need the Spotify URI or Apple ID of the song, these can be received from your distributor sometimes 4 weeks in advance. Once you have these details you can create a pre-save gate using one of the services mentioned in the Gates chapter.

Once the song is closer to release you may be able to paste the URI in the Spotify search bar - you will be able to see the artwork and track title, though you won't be able to play the song until the official release date. Instead you will see the songs grayed out, this is fine, the good news is that the save button will be available to click. Fans can 'save' your song to their Spotify library, meaning that as soon as your song goes live it is already in their saved section. This makes them feel warm and tingly knowing they can hear your song first. The other cool thing is, that even though the songs are grayed out, users can still drag the song into their favorite playlist, meaning as soon as the song goes live it is already in a bunch of your fans playlists!

"

Tip: In the Spotify desktop app, go to the 'Settings' menu and select 'Show unavailable songs in playlists'. This will show you songs that aren't live yet (grayed out), so you can see if your song has been placed in a playlist before it goes live (release day). You can also use this as a curator to drag a song into your playlist in the days before it goes live. Go to New Music Friday for another country that is ahead of you (earlier timezone) and you will see this in action.

Influencer marketing

From a quiet kid with a cool camera who takes great videos, to Dwayne "The Rock" Johnson, influencers can be anyone. An influencer is someone with a large following... but more importantly, they have a collection of engaged followers who who listen to what they have to say. Earlier in this book you were told to sign up with Instagram - if you have not yet done this, sign up now... I will wait.

Here's some homework. Go on Instagram, find some people who share your passion outside of music. If you like video games, search the hashtag #videogames and find someone with a large following and lots of engagement on their posts. Take the time to follow 20 of these influencers and write meaningful comments on their posts. I don't mean "nice video, I want to play that game". Be specific. Let's say they posted a video of them playing Grand Theft Auto V, comment and say "hey, I just finished the game with Trevor and found it was really tough, but I thought his ending was a much better story than the other two... do you think he will return in the next GTA?". What you've done is show that you have paid attention to their video, made a thoughtful comment and asked for their opinion.

Now comes the exciting part, turn on notifications for Instagram and be ready. If they respond to your comment (you'll get notified because they will tag you in their reply), then respond immediately while they are active on the app and engaged, your notification will be bumped to the top. If you are lucky enough to get another response then ask them if you can send them a quick DM or email because you want to keep chatting and "don't want to get lost in the comments" or something along those lines.

Once you are in the DM, don't talk about yourself, just keep engaging them and asking great questions. This is developing the relationship. If you play it cool you may find they follow you back (which is why it's important to never be fake in your social media profiles). After they follow you back it's time to ask them a little more about themselves, such as, "how long have you been a gamer", "do you have other hobbies you enjoy". Once they respond you will likely get a response follow by "... how about yourself?". Now is when you tell them in two sentences what you are about. "Avid gamer from California, loved Nintendo but I'm now all about PS4, also make electronic music and dream to have a song featured in a video game". Now you have let them know that you also create music, you invite them to respond if they are interested.

Now be careful, it's still possible to scare them off. If they ask to hear some of your music, don't send them multiple links and DMs, breathe and pick your best song that represents your sound. Tell them a little about the track you send them so they know what to prepare for, "it's a deep electronic chill track that reminds me of driving home after a long day".

Now leave them to listen. If you haven't heard from them, but see they have posted new content online, it would be good to comment on the next post, without mentioning your music.

There is a good chance that if you give them enough time and then follow up (say 2 weeks), they will think you are chill and be more likely to respond. If they show any interest in your music here's the cool part. Tell them that you would be happy to send them a copy of your song to use for free in any of their videos. This also means that you now have a chance to get your music in front of their audience.

If they bite, be sure to send links to your social media with an easy download link (Dropbox or Google Drive). This gives them everything they need, you will most likely see your artist and song title in the video description as well as perhaps a tag in the comments and a link to your socials (which is why short links are important because Instagram doesn't allow clickable links). In other words, people only see the text version e.g. johnsmithmusic.com or bit.ly/johnsmithmusic, neither is clickable but people are likely to remember and type the text into their web browser.

The YouTube follower hack

This is a very simple hack to encourage new visitors to subscribe to your YouTube channel via a popup that will ask them if they want to subscribe. Keep in mind that clicking subscribe takes the same amount of energy as closing this small popup. While not everyone may subscribe when prompted, making it easier for them will give you a better chance.

To create a link you simply need to take an existing YouTube URL e.g.

http://www.youtube.com/askmikewarner

Now simply add *?sub_confirmation=1* to the end of the URL e.g.

http://www.youtube.com/askmikewarner?sub_confirmation =1

Now, you've most likely subscribed to your YouTube channel already which means if you test the follow URL with ?sub_confirmation=1 included the popup will not show. You can get past this by opening a private tab in your web browser and then entering the URL. If this doesn't work you can unsubscribe to your channel and then test the link to see the subscribe popup.

Anywhere you share your link to your YouTube channel you can use the full URL to grow your followers. Add it to your website, email signature, social media posts and profiles...

literally every time you share the link to your channel use this new URL instead.

If the new URL is a little long remember you can use a URL shortener.

Spotify time jump

This is a fun discovery I made while reviewing Spotify shortcuts. It helps you get to the key part of a song. This is particularly useful when showing your song to a curator, who may only listen for 15 seconds (if you are lucky). This lets you share a link which when opened will play the song at the exact point you want the curator to hear, perhaps the chorus or a kick ass guitar solo, depending on what the curator will be most responsive to.

Now, if you want to see this in action you can type the following into the search bar in Spotify, then press enter.

spotify:track:7Dbg5O9nNWu6SWxDjJ9qoq#3:40

The URI above is followed by #3:40 with 3:40 being the time in minutes and seconds into the track you want it to begin playing from.

The above example is Phil Collins - In The Air Tonight, 3 minutes and 40 seconds in is when the drums start.

Use this to your advantage and pitch the best part of your song first.

The Facebook birthday post

Now I can't take credit for being the first to think of this but it's too brilliant not to share. This can be applied to promote a playlist, new song, or to get some follows on a new artist profile.

If you have a birthday coming up on Facebook (don't be cheeky and change it), then follow these steps.

Go to privacy Settings, Timeline and Tagging, change 'Who can post on your timeline?' to 'Only me'.

People will be notified of your birthday a few days in advance so post early, also remembering that some of your friends may be located elsewhere in the world being one day ahead of you.

Post a new profile photo with a great shot of yourself (keeping it real). In the photo description mention how amazing it would be if everyone could follow your new playlist, save your new single, or follow your artist profile.

Facebook will notify all your friends that it is your birthday, when they go to post on your wall there will be no option to do a new post so they will comment on your most recent post (in this case, your profile photo).

All of these comments and likes on your new photo will generate high engagement with your post, meaning it will appear in more of your friends' news feeds.

Keep in mind that your Facebook profile is about you, a real person, so try to include a story with the photo to make it more interesting. E.g. a photo of you on a hike with the description "Feeling on top of the world here at X mountain, super excited to now have my music on X, follow me here [link]." If you are feeling extra clever, use a short link.

Keep selling CDs

CDs are an additional revenue stream. I compare it to the feeling of going into a store and buying a product, it makes you feel good. Fans go to a show, or participate in a sale to buy a CD to make them feel good. They may never listen (or even unwrap) the CD but the purchase part of the process felt good, knowing that the money went to the Artist.

What happens next is the fan gets in their car, or drives home and then starts streaming that very same album via a streaming service. The artist now has revenue from the CD sale (let's say $5 profit per CD) as well as from the streaming service.

I definitely don't recommend just handing out CDs for free to everyone you meet as it can cause people to not see value in your music. If someone pays for something, even a few $ they are more likely to make time to listen, or at least keep it in their car, on their bookshelf etc. That CD may one day be passed on to a friend with a "listen to this", which is word of mouth marketing.

Want to increase the value of your CD, make sure you sign it for the fan, if there is a personal message with their name on there it's safe to assume they will keep this and possibly also take a photo and share on social media.

When looking at CD manufacturers, keep in mind that size matters. If you use full size jewel cases for your CDs the price of postage will increase, plus the risk of the case being cracked during transit, lastly it doesn't fit into a jacket pocket as easily.

I suggest looking at thin cardboard sleeves, some distributors call these eco packs, which as the name suggests are also good for the environment which is a bonus. Fans will be more likely to purchase these if they easily fit in their pocket.

Say thank you

This may seem like an odd thing to mention but always say thank you. It takes less than one second to say and can be the difference between someone feeling happy with their decision to support you, or feel like they were not important enough to be thanked (or you didn't value their support) and you will most likely not hear from them again.

If someone really helps you early in your career, don't ever forget them. Find a way to thank them. I had a friend who runs a large independent playlist network and he helped me immensely both through supporting my music and with advice when it came to building my own playlists.

This started as a thank you, then led to me booking a flight when he was speaking at a conference, in another city. I shouted him a few beers (shouting means buying in Australia). Years later and we are now good friends and still share music, tips and I even curate a playlist for his hugely successful brand. That man's name is Carlos and he is the founder of Indiemono, one of the largest independent playlist brands on Spotify, with over 1 million followers across all of their playlists.

So, always say thank you. Remember those who supported you from the start. You never know where they may be in a few years time. If one of you grows, you both grow.

Here's some suggestions for different ways to say thank you.

- Share the playlist as your 'artist pick' on your Spotify profile, do this at artists.spotify.com

- Tweet and tag the curator, telling everyone to go check out their playlist

- Post a brief video of you "in the studio" thanking the curator for adding your song.

❝

Tip: If you take a screenshot of a curators playlist, be sure to click 'follow' first so it shows that you are following and listening to their playlist. This makes the 'thank you' more genuine and will likely receive a more positive response from the curator.

Find more curators

Now that you are starting to make some strong connections with curators, the next step is to find ways to connect with others through them, sometimes it is as simple as asking nicely. With these examples it is important to put your own touch on the conversations / emails.

Ask for an introduction

Once you have built rapport and have a curator that you speak with a few times per month, it's ok to ask them the following question, I've even drafted an example for you:

"Hi [NAME], it's been a pleasure sharing music with you these last few months and so happy to be able to support your music as well. I was wondering if you have any other contacts that would be interested in a similar type of arrangement? I'd be happy to introduce you to some of my contacts in return, as I am sure we could help each other through facilitated introductions".

In this email I have explained why I am asking for other contacts (because I know the value of a larger network), while also offering an introduction to my contacts (something of value in return).

If you are asked to introduce one of your contacts, ask them directly first to make sure they are ok with this. You don't want to upset your existing contacts who are already happily sharing music with you.

What if a curator leaves their job?

If you have developed a relationship with a curator and they have advised that they are leaving their job you should follow these steps:

Make yourself aware of the circumstances, if they are leaving their record label job to pursue their music career you can assume they are leaving on good terms.

Wish them all the best and ask if you could keep in touch as you'd love to hear about their next moves. You never know, they could move on to a bigger role in a similar company and you'll be glad they gave you their personal email/cell.

Once they have acknowledged your well wishes and shown they are happy to keep in touch, you can ask them if it's possible to be introduced to their successor as you would love to continue sharing music with them as well.

There is nothing more valuable than a personal introduction, especially when it is from the previous staff member. It's like meeting a friend of a friend, there is instantly a level of comfort and trust involved, it's on you to build it from there.

❝

Tip: When engagement with a contact is at its peak (or after you have exchanged more than a couple of nice emails) it is a good time to connect on LinkedIn. A connection request on LinkedIn is far less invasive and more accepted in the early stage of a new relationship with a curator. The best part about requesting a new connection on LinkedIn, is that you will be notified if they move on to another role or get promoted - the platform is also a great way to continue reaching them via messaging.

Out of office responses

This is the next best thing to an introduction. Let's say you email your playlist curator at record label X and you receive an out of office response. There's little chance they are going to reply or place your song but there is a very high chance they will include an alternative contact (or contacts) to reach out to in their absence. This is the perfect time to do a self introduction. Here's an example of how I would reach out, please rewrite in your own words.

"Hello [NAME],

I usually share new music with John and I know that he is currently on holiday in Hawaii (1), which I am extremely jealous of. I was told that you may be the best person to contact in his absence and just wanted to reach out as I have new music to share if possible? (2)

If you are not the best contact for this, could you please point me towards them and I will be sure to spare your inbox of my musical pitches. (3)

All the best,
Michael"

It was important that I know John, and well enough to know that he is on holiday in Hawaii. This will likely cause the recipient to keep reading.

I didn't pitch in the email. I asked for permission, which is very important because if this email goes to the wrong person and there is a bunch of song links they are likely to just move it to the "I don't have time for this" basket.

Lastly, I gave them an opportunity to push me towards someone else, another contact, maybe a better contact for what I am looking for.

If they respond positively, hit them with your song pitch and use a little charm. If all goes well you may just have another contact at that record label.

If they respond with another contact you should reach out to, follow the process again and introduce yourself to the new contact, summarizing your initial contact, how you know them and that the second contact suggested you should connect with them.

Case studies

In addition to pitching my own music, I have worked closely with artists and their managers to apply these practices and help further their careers. These case studies show where growth for the specific artists came from and how it was achieved, as well as the follow ups to allow for future opportunities.

Hello Harry & Thomas Garcia - Tea & Poetry

Spotify:
https://open.spotify.com/track/5t69tqvNJRjRzjJ844M3uG

Apple Music:
https://itunes.apple.com/us/album/you-me-single/1360297753

Tea & Poetry is a collaboration between two electronic music producers from LA.

Added to Starbucks Coffeehouse Playlist

This was pure luck, the song had 'tea' in the title and was noticed by a friend of the Starbucks music team. Follow up was extremely important, this was done by reaching out on LinkedIn and Twitter to first say thank you, then ask if more music can be submitted. Email addresses were offered and as a result future songs pitched have been supported. The song was also added to a second Starbucks playlist 9 months later.

Added to Fresh Finds: Hiptronix

Spotify editorial team still use other methods to discover new music and artists. Blogs are still relevant and Hype Machine gathers some of the most active, trusted and engaged blogs together into one convenient website with charts for each genre. This song was pitched to a blog called AcidStag (pitched through SubmitHub). AcidStag added the song to their Friday playlist and did a blog post, which then got the song onto Hype Machine. The next week it appeared in Fresh Finds: Hiptronix.

Both artists went from less than 1,000 streams on all of their previous releases and 100 monthly listeners to peaking at 100,000 monthly listeners on their profiles and the song currently has 220,000 streams on Spotify.

Date Night - Date Night (self titled album)

Spotify:
https://open.spotify.com/album/2qqqqSuv2iKyfUdxn8yWrM

Apple Music:
https://itunes.apple.com/us/album/date-night/1164749906

Self titled debut album from Australian electronic group Date Night.

Added to the New Releases section on Spotify Australia

This was the result of reaching out through Twitter to the social media team. An initial tweet was short and sweet, introducing ourselves as Australian natives and asking if we can get a follow back to DM them a preview of our debut album. We received a response with an email address to pitch to the Australian music team and an invitation to send through a link to the album. We did both and the week of our album was released we were featured on the New Releases page. This led to multiple playlist adds, saves of the album and followers.

Added to Fresh Electronic on Spotify

At the time of writing Austin Kramer is the head of Electronic Music on Spotify and without a doubt the most important person to pitch to for any EDM artist. A song add to Fresh Electronic or Mint could be enough to kickstart an artists career. Previously Austin Kramer had a pitch form (bit.ly/kramify) which was the only way to send music to him, this has since been removed. Now, the only way to send unreleased music (any genre) for consideration is directly through (see 'Pitch directly to the Spotify editorial team').

Added by Apple Music to New Music Monday

What started as a LinkedIn conversation, led to multiple emails and email introductions. The key is to always acknowledge anyone that is included in the 'CC' field of an email and be sure to thank everyone involved. Following up from this 'Forget' was added to New Music Monday. 100,000 streams were gained as a result of this.

Payola

Payola (sometimes also referred to as playola) is paying someone to add your song to their playlist. While this may sound tempting let's look at some reasons as to why it is a terrible idea.

- Payola is against most streaming services terms and conditions.

- Spotify actively seeks out curators who ask for money in turn for placements and those curators are getting shut down, losing all their followers and getting a bad name for themselves.

- If an artist participates in payola they risk any opportunities for support from editorial teams at streaming services, as well as being blacklisted, which means their music is completely removed from a streaming service... sometimes forever.

Still not scared? Do a quick web search for payola and you'll see many reports of artists being blacklisted, losing their fans and revenue, and being looked down on by their peers. Plus by the end of this book you shouldn't need payola, you should be crushing it organically.

DON'T DO IT!

Final thoughts

This book was a long time coming. I really wanted to share everything I wish I had known when I started out. The industry is changing constantly and I'm always learning. This book will continue to be updated and revised, and I will continue to share even more knowledge in the future.

Since the first release in 2018 this book has already been revised. A lot has changed in the music streaming world but a lot has changed for me as well. This book has opened doors for me to participate in conference panels, host live workshops, appear on various podcasts, and even my first live interview on TV (with CNBC's Jon Fortt). None of this would have been possible if it wasn't for the amazing support I have received... whether it was a tweet, email, or even just telling a friend. I feel a huge level of responsibility to make sure I continue delivering current and reliable information to help further your career.

The music industry is an ever evolving landscape. As this is the first edition of the book, please don't hold back if there's something you feel is lacking, or if you would like me to expand on or update specific topics in a future edition.

Go out there, keep creating, keep learning and keep sharing.

Thanks for reading.

Mike Warner

@askmikewarner
AskMikeWarner.com
WorkHardPlaylistHard.com

Credits

Book cover art by Spectator Jonze
spectatorjonze.com

Edited by Sue Oreszczyn and Ranya Khoury

Words by Mike Warner

More learning

Here are other books I have read and recommend, as well as online courses that I have personally participated in and benefited from.

Books

How to Make It In The New Music Business
Ari Herstand

The Slotify Method
George Goodrich

All You Need to Know About the Music Business
Donald Passman

Courses

Music Industry Blueprint Masterclass
Rick Barker

Fanbase Blueprint
Rick Barker

Affiliate Program

If you found value from this book and would like to earn some extra money by sharing a link with your friends and fellow artists, why not become an affiliate.

Visit workhardplaylisthard.com / affiliate for more details!

Testimonials

❝

"My friend Mike is my go to for streaming advice mainly because he comes from music and the music I like and not just a statistics type knowledge, but that special touch and feel for where a track can work well. His playlists are always put together in an organic way, not just strategy - they are solid musically. I have seen him grow from one playlist to a massive operation over the years."
StoneBridge (Grammy nominated producer and remixer)

❝

"Mike knows the streaming world extremely well and as an artist has a unique view on the sector too. With a proven track record of success this book is a must read for anyone interested in this space."
Kieron Donoghue (Founder of Humble Angel Records)

❝

"What impresses me most about Mike is that his knowledge of the digital music world is born from a true love for music (unfortunately not always the case in the biz these days). From

both an artist and industry perspective, Mike always seems to be up on the trends and is always looking to find new ways to expose not only his groups music, but the music of other talented artists from around the world to wider audiences. Beyond his clear expertise in the areas that he works, he also just happens to be a great person to deal with, talk to and collaborate with. Nothing but respect for his hustle and know how."

Brian Delaney (Tommy Boy Records)

"

"It still amazes me how much Mike knows about the streaming world.. although it makes complete sense. He's constantly looking for new endeavors to expand his knowledge about the digital music sector. Whether it's curating a playlist network, growing his own artist profile, recording informational podcasts or speaking at conferences - Mike clearly has a keen eye for all things music. Over a few months time, I've been able to watch his own projects grow substantially - showcasing his ability to provide top-notch advice that holds value."

Ranya Khoury (Hits Magazine)

Glossary

DJ

Disc Jockey. Can apply to anyone that is in control of the music, from a Radio jockey to a Turntablist, or a person that plays recorded music using equipment.

DM

Direct message. This is sending a private message to someone through social media for example in Facebook, Twitter or Instagram you will send a Direct Message.

ISRC

International Standard Recording Code.

MUZAK

Muzak is a brand of background music played in retail stores and other public establishments.